SCRIPTURAL PRAYERS
FOR THE
PRAYING TEEN

SCRIPTURAL PRAYERS
FOR THE
PRAYING TEEN

Transform Your Life
Through Powerful Prayer

WHITE STONE BOOKS

TULSA, OKLAHOMA

All Scripture quotations are taken from the *King James Version* of the Bible.

06 05 04 03   10 9 8 7 6 5 4 3 2 1

Scriptural Prayers for the Praying Teen
ISBN 1-59379-003-1
Copyright © 2003 by Word and Spirit Resources
P.O. Box 700311
Tulsa, OK 74170

Published by White Stone Books
P.O. Box 35035
Tulsa, OK 74153

Contents

I. My Relationship With God

II. My Purpose in Life

III. **My Spiritual Growth**

V. When I Face...

VI. My Relationships

VII. My Every Day

VIII. My Nation

1

My Relationship With God

Start the Day With God

Lord, thanks for the gift of this day. You made this day, and I will enjoy it to its fullest. I thank You, Lord, that Your mercy and grace are new every morning.

I rejoice because I am Your child. I have been filled with Your Spirit. You are so much greater than anyone in the world. Holy Spirit, You are bigger than any problem, obstacle, calamity, or challenge that might be ahead of me today.

Lord, I thank You for the wonderful gift that You have provided in giving me this day. My gift back to You is what I do with this day for Your glory. Help me to honor You in all that I do today. I acknowledge You and praise You today. It's so good to know that You have promised to direct my steps, to order my life.

Let my friends, classmates, teachers, coworkers, and family see You in me today. Help me to say things that are full of Your grace. Help me to be a blessing to the people around me. Help me to bring Your light, hope, and encouragement to everyone I see today.

Lord, no matter what happens today, I trust You to see me through. Your Word says that I can do all things through Christ who strengthens me. Since You are on my side, no one can be against me. Thanks for Your favor in every area of my life today.

Scriptures

This is the day which the Lord hath made; we will rejoice and be glad in it (Psalm 118:24).

It is of the Lord's mercies that we are not consumed, because his compassions fail not. They are new every morning: great is thy faithfulness (Lamentations 3:22,23).

In all thy ways acknowledge him, and he shall direct thy paths (Proverbs 3:6).

Let no corrupt communication proceed out of your mouth, but that which is good to the use of edifying, that it may minister grace unto the hearers (Ephesians 4:29).

I can do all things through Christ which strengtheneth me (Philippians 4:13).

What shall we then say to these things? If God be for us, who can be against us? (Romans 8:31).

Dwelling in the Secret Place

Lord, help me to walk into the place of Your presence. Help me to come into the place of rest and peace that I can find only in Your presence.

Lord, I want to live in Your secret place so I will remain safe and secure under Your shadow. You are my refuge and my fortress, God. I lean and rely on You, and I confidently place my trust in You. I thank You that You deliver me from every trap that the devil would try to disable me with. I thank You that You cover me with Your wings of protection, and under those wings I find a safe haven. Your truth and Your faithfulness are my shield.

Because of Your divine protection in my life, I am not afraid of attempts at causing terror or the evil plots and lies of the wicked. I am not afraid of the diseases, destruction, calamity, or sudden death that the enemy would try to attack me with.

A thousand may fall at my side and ten thousand at my right hand, but it shall not, will not, and cannot come near me, because I am inaccessible in the secret place of the Most High.

Scriptures

He that dwelleth in the secret place of the most High shall abide under the shadow of the Almighty (Psalm 91:1).

And they that know thy name will put their trust in thee: for thou, Lord, hast not forsaken them that seek thee (Psalm 91:10).

A thousand may fall at your side, ten thousand at your right hand, but it will not come near you (Psalm 91:7).

Exalting the Lord

Lord, worshiping You gives me strength and frees my soul to soar like an eagle. Being in Your presence gives me joy and makes me feel so happy. In Your presence I find peace that makes no sense to my mind because it's there even when life gets really tough. Your grace and mercy heal my heart. Your forgiveness cleans my soul.

Lord, You are my rock and fortress. You rule my ways. You faithfully lead me down Your paths of righteousness and prosperity for Your glory in the earth. You free me from every trap that is set before me. You are my refuge and hiding place from trouble. My heart is filled with joy because of Your love for me. You saw me in my hour of need, understood the stress in my mind, and refused to let the enemy take control of my life. Because of Your deep love for me, Lord, You took up my case and rescued me from my past. You set me in a big land of prosperity, and in Your presence I will enjoy Your blessings forever.

Scriptures

But they that wait upon the Lord shall renew their strength; they shall mount up with wings as eagles; they shall run, and not be weary; and they shall walk, and not faint (Isaiah 40:31).

Thou hast made known to me the ways of life; thou shalt make me full of joy with thy countenance (Acts 2:28).

And the peace of God, which passeth all understanding, shall keep your hearts and minds through Christ Jesus (Philippians 4:7).

For thou art my rock and my fortress; therefore for thy name's sake lead me, and guide me (Psalm 31:3).

He restoreth my soul: he leadeth me in the paths of righteousness for his name's sake (Psalm 23:3).

God's Love for Me

Father God, in Jesus' name, I thank You for Your love that is so great that You did not hold back Your own Son but gave Him up as a sacrifice to bring me to You. Your love is the greatest force in the world.

I thank You that nothing can separate me from Your love—not difficulties, stress, persecution, famine, danger, or battle. Lord, Your love is the rock and foundation of my life. No matter what situation I face, no matter what challenges come, Your love will keep me going.

I am more than a conqueror because of Your love in me. I know for sure that nothing can separate me from Your love—not death, life, angels, demons, threats, things to come, powers, heights, or depths. Nothing in all creation can separate me from Your love, which is in Christ Jesus my Lord.

Scriptures

He that spared not his own Son, but delivered him up for us all, how shall he not with him also freely give us all things? (Romans 8:32).

Who shall separate us from the love of Christ? shall tribulation, or distress, or persecution, or famine, or nakedness, or peril, or sword? (Romans 8:35).

Nay, in all these things we are more than conquerors through him that loved us (Romans 8:37).

The Greater One in Me

I thank You, Lord, that You are greater than anything in the world. Lord, You are greater than Satan and the forces of darkness. You are greater than sin, sickness, and disease. You are greater than want and need. You are greater than any circumstance I might face. You are greater than any obstacle that comes up before me. You are greater than any challenge that comes into my life. Lord, You are greater than my own doubts, insecurities, or uncertainties. You are greater than anything this life can throw at me.

I am more than a conqueror through You, Lord. I can face the circumstances of life boldly and confidently because You're with me everywhere I go. You are greater, and You live in me. You put me over, You make me successful, and with You I cannot fail!

Scriptures

Ye are of God, little children, and have overcome them: because greater is he that is in you, than he that is in the world (1 John 4:4).

These things I have spoken unto you, that in me ye might have peace. In the world ye shall have tribulation: but be of good cheer; I have overcome the world (John 16:33).

Nay, in all these things we are more than conquerors through him that loved us (Romans 8:37).

The Lord Is My Refuge

Thank You, Lord, that Your Word says that You are my refuge and strong tower. You are my fortress and place of security and safety. Help me to live in that place of confidence and peace.

Because I have made You my refuge and my home, no evil can touch me; no disease or tragedy can come near me. You send Your angels to walk with me, defend me, and preserve me in all my ways. Wherever I go and whatever I do, Your angels go with me to protect me from harm, injury, and evil.

Even though I may walk in the midst of danger, it will have no effect on me. Because You love me, You will deliver me and put me in a high place. Because I have made You my refuge, Your mercy, grace, and kindness surround me like a cloud. I will call upon You, and You will answer me. You will be with me in times of trouble, and You will deliver me and honor me. With a long life, You satisfy me and show me Your salvation.

In that place of refuge, I receive Your wisdom and insight. In that place of refuge, I hear Your voice clearly and receive direction and guidance for every area of my life. Thank You for being my refuge, in Jesus' name.

Scriptures

The name of the Lord is a strong tower; the righteous run to it and are safe (Proverbs 18:10).

There shall no evil befall thee, neither shall any plague come nigh thy dwelling, for he shall give his angels charge over thee, to keep thee in all thy ways (Psalm 91:10,11).

With long life will I satisfy him and show him my salvation (Psalm 91:16).

Teach me to do your will, for you are my God; may your good Spirit lead me on level ground (Psalm 143:10).

Joy in the Lord

I thank You, Lord, that You made today, and I am going to enjoy it! I rejoice because once I was lost, but now I am found. Once I was blind, but now I see. Once I was on my way to hell, but now I am on my way to heaven.

Lord, I will rejoice because Your love has redeemed me from destruction and has filled me with Your righteousness. I can rejoice today because You promised to never leave me or forsake me.

Help me to rejoice in the middle of difficult times. Help me to keep my mind focused on You and Your Word even in the middle of conflict. Help me to realize that my joy is not based on the circumstances around me but is the result of Your presence within me. So I can always rejoice and shout for joy. Because You love me, You want me to be blessed and fulfilled in every part of my life. You are a great and wonderful God, and I will rejoice in Your name forever.

Scriptures

I will be glad and rejoice in thee: I will sing praise to thy name, O thou most High (Psalm 9:2).

Let the redeemed of the Lord say so, whom he hath redeemed from the hand of the enemy (Psalm 107:2).

Then he said unto them, Go your way, eat the fat, and drink the sweet, and send portions unto them for whom nothing is prepared: for this day is holy unto our Lord: neither be ye sorry; for the joy of the Lord is your strength (Nehemiah 8:10).

Relationship With God

In everything, my relationship with You comes first. You are everything to me. You are the beginning and the end of everything. You are the great I Am. I give You glory and honor through my entire life. I am nothing; You are everything. I will seek You forever and ever. Every day that I live will be dedicated to You. And when I see You in heaven, I will join with the angels and sing, "Holy, holy, holy" to Your name.

I'm going to seek You in public places like church, school, and Bible studies. I'm going to seek You in my quiet times when You and I can sit alone and talk about our relationship. And I'm going to seek You through every day of life.

Everything about You is beautiful. Just to look upon Your face is amazing. Being in Your presence is better than a thousand days anywhere else. Even through time with my friends and family, I will seek You, Lord. With all that is within me, I will lift up Your awesome, holy name. The Lord Jesus is my God, and I want the whole world to know it.

Scriptures

I am Alpha and Omega, the beginning and the ending, saith the Lord, which is, and which was, and which is to come, the Almighty (Revelation 1:8).

And God said unto Moses, I AM THAT I AM: and he said, Thus shalt thou say unto the children of Israel, I AM hath sent me unto you (Exodus 3:14).

And one cried unto another, and said, Holy, holy, holy, is the Lord of hosts: the whole earth is full of his glory (Isaiah 6:3).

Better is one day in your courts than a thousand elsewhere; I would rather be a doorkeeper in the house of my God than dwell in the tents of the wicked (Psalm 84:10).

When I Feel Like God Is Far Away

Lord, sometimes it seems as if You are so far away. Lately I feel as if my prayers are without power and the cares of this world have choked my spiritual vitality.

Lord, renew in me Your joy and strength. Give me back the joy of my salvation. By faith I receive Your love and mercy. No matter what I feel like, I know that You will never leave me or forsake me. By faith I encourage myself in You, Lord. I sing praises and songs to You. I worship and adore You, Lord—not because of how I feel but because of who You are and my love for You. I am persuaded that nothing can separate me from Your love—not death, not life, not angels, not demons, not powers, not the present or the future, not heights, nor depths, and not any creature.

I am alive to You, Lord. Your joy is my strength. I trust You. Your goodness and mercy fill my life till they spill out of me and change the environment and the people around me.

Let Your love, joy, and peace rule my life. Strengthen me by Your power.

Scriptures

And the cares of this world, and the deceitfulness of riches, and the lusts of other things entering in, choke the word, and it becometh unfruitful (Mark 4:19).

Restore unto me the joy of thy salvation; and uphold me with thy free spirit (Psalm 51:12).

Let your conversation be without covetousness; and be content with such things as ye have: for he hath said, I will never leave thee, nor forsake thee (Hebrews 13:5).

Let the word of Christ dwell in you richly in all wisdom; teaching and admonishing one another in psalms and hymns and spiritual songs, singing with grace in your hearts to the Lord (Colossians 3:16).

For I am persuaded, that neither death, nor life, nor angels, nor principalities, nor powers, nor things present, nor things to come, nor height, nor depth, nor any other creature, shall be able to separate us from the love of God, which is in Christ Jesus our Lord (Romans 8:38,39).

End the Day With God

Lord, as I come to You at the end of this day, I thank You for being faithful to me. Thanks for providing for me. Thanks for being with me and protecting me. Thanks for Your blessings in every area of my life.

Holy Spirit, show me anything that I may have said or done that was displeasing to You, so that I can repent for it and receive Your forgiveness. If I caused harm or injury to anyone, I ask You to forgive me and to heal their hurts.

Now help me to not worry or be frustrated about any mistakes I made today. I give You all the cares and concerns of today's events. I forget the past and look toward tomorrow. Lord, thanks for the peace that lives in my heart. Thank You, Lord, that tomorrow is a new day. I thank You that no matter how many times I messed up today I can start fresh and new in You tomorrow. Thanks for helping me to follow You.

I trust You to fulfill Your plans and purposes in me. Lord, thanks for designing my future. Thanks for a restful night's sleep, in Jesus' name.

Scriptures

Casting all your care upon him; for he careth for you (1 Peter 5:7).

It is of the Lord's mercies that we are not consumed, because his compassions fail not. They are new every morning: great is thy faithfulness (Lamentations 3:22,23).

I will lie down and sleep in peace, for you alone, O Lord, make me dwell in safety (Psalm 4:8).

II

My Purpose in Life

Discovering My Purpose

Lord Jesus, I am searching for meaning in my life. Sometimes I get so confused about where to go or what to do. I ask You, Lord, in Your divine time, to reveal these things to me.

I know that Your plans for me are for good and not for evil. I know that Your plans are designed to bring me a hope and a future. I am nothing without You, Lord. Everything that I could ever hope to be is found in You alone. Help me in my search for purpose to find You and to not be led astray by the other voices that I hear.

Help me to not be stressed about my direction, but in everything to seek Your guidance. I make the commitment to place my future in Your hands. Only You know what is best for me. Bring godly friends to my side to help confirm the words that You place in my heart.

I do not ask these things out of selfishness or ambition, but just so that You will be glorified through my life. Let Your glory and Your love show through me in my purpose.

Scriptures

For I know the thoughts that I think toward you, saith the Lord, thoughts of peace, and not of evil, to give you an expected end (Jeremiah 29:11).

Trust in the Lord with all thine heart; and lean not unto thine own understanding. In all thy ways acknowledge him, and he shall direct thy paths (Proverbs 3:5,6).

The Lord will fulfill his purpose for me; your love, O Lord, endures forever... (Psalm 138:8).

God Working in Me

You, Lord, light my way before me. You give me clear instruction and keep me firmly on the paths of righteousness. I claim victory over the enemy. Your Word is always before me. It is tested, tried, and true. I put my complete trust in You. You are my shield and my refuge. You are my rock and my fortress. You are my hiding place and strong tower.

You enlighten me with Your understanding concerning the plan You have for my life. You have set me free from all obstacles. You have made me secure and capable in You. I maintain a steadfast resistance to the attacks of the enemy, and I live in a place of blessing and prominence because of Your love for me.

Your Spirit leads and directs my steps. He is my helper and my friend. He gives me wisdom, insight, and clarity concerning the decisions I have to make. Your wisdom and counsel give me a firm foundation for my faith. By Your Word, Your truth is established in my heart and brings strength and stability to my life.

Lord, work in me and through me to fulfill Your plan and purpose for my life. Use me to minister Your love to my friends, teachers, parents, siblings, and everyone else in my life. As I acknowledge and worship You, I thank You that You direct and guide my steps.

Scriptures

He restoreth my soul: he leadeth me in the paths of righteousness for his name's sake (Psalm 23:3).

The Lord is my rock, and my fortress, and my deliverer; my God, my strength, in whom I will trust; my buckler, and the horn of my salvation, and my high tower (Psalm 18:2).

Likewise the Spirit also helpeth our infirmities: for we know not what we should pray for as we ought: but the Spirit itself maketh intercession for us with groanings which cannot be uttered (Romans 8:26).

Setting Priorities

Lord, help me to make sure that I spend the right amount of time on the things that are the most important, and to spend less time on the things that aren't. First of all, help me to always keep You as my top priority, which everything else in my life follows. I don't just want You to be first in my life; I want You to be first, second, third, fourth, fifth, sixth, and so on. I want everything in my life to just be a result of my relationship with You.

Lord, help me to keep my family as a top priority. Help me to not forget what You have given me in a family. Help me to keep my schoolwork as a priority. I know that You want me to be diligent in everything and make sure that I get done what needs to be done. Help me to also keep my friends as a priority. Let me not forget the importance of other people in my life.

Give me wisdom on what to spend my time on. Help me to find the right balance and to know what activities to keep and what activities to throw out.

Scriptures

But seek ye first the kingdom of God, and his righteousness; and all these things shall be added unto
you (Matthew 6:33).

If any of you lack wisdom, let him ask of God, that
giveth to all men liberally, and upbraideth not;
and it shall be given him (James 1:5).

A man's heart deviseth his way: but the Lord
directeth his steps (Proverbs 16:9).

Right Motives

Lord, I pray that everything that I do would be to glorify Your name. I ask that You would help me to never get off track or do things out of the wrong attitude. The only reason I am on the planet is that You said so.

Help me to not fall into pride. Help me to know that You are the author and the finisher of my faith, and that my best choice is to give You my life. I ask that You would humble me when I need to be humbled and show me more of Your heart.

Help me to not fall into deceit. I don't need that to sustain me. When I want something a certain way, give me the strength to not accept a counterfeit but to give the situation to You. I found that when I try to do things without You, that is where I get into trouble.

Give me a clean, humble heart. Try me and see every anxious thought that I might have. Remove from me every evil thing, and lead me in Your everlasting ways.

Scriptures

Looking unto Jesus the author and finisher of our faith; who for the joy that was set before him endured the cross, despising the shame, and is set down at the right hand of the throne of God (Hebrews 12:2).

Create in me a clean heart, O God; and renew a right spirit within me (Psalm 51:10).

Search me, O God, and know my heart; test me and know my anxious thoughts. See if there is any offensive way in me, and lead me in the way everlasting (Psalm 139:23,24).

Staying in the Will of God

I don't want to be outside of Your plans, Lord. In Your plans there is hope, love, and everlasting joy. That's where I want to be. Help me to avoid things that get me away from that. Why would I want to trade all that is in Your will for something else? I don't know, but at times I have made decisions where that is exactly what I do. Keep me strong. Holy Spirit, continue to remind me of all that is found in Your arms. Make it obvious to me which decisions will lead me off track.

Give me the patience to stick with You even when times get rough. Even when my friends make decisions that are out of Your will, help me to stand firm. I make that commitment to You, Jesus.

Thank You that Your will lists me as a beneficiary. I am so grateful because I am not worthy of such an honor. But You are such an awesome God to give that right to me. Help me to stay under Your will and to not fall away.

Scriptures

And see if there be any wicked way in me, and lead me in the way everlasting (Psalm 139:24).

Shew me thy ways, O Lord; teach me thy paths (Psalm 25:4).

Giving thanks unto the Father, which hath made us meet to be partakers of the inheritance of the saints in light (Colossians 1:12).

Doors of Opportunity

Lord, I pray that the positions that You want me to be in will be available for me. I ask that You would place me exactly in those places. Lord, if You want me to be in a certain job, thank You that the employer will hire me. And if You want me to take a certain trip or go to a certain school, thank You that I will be accepted. You are so awesome in the way that You work things out.

And, Lord, if I am not supposed to be in certain situations, keep the doors shut. Even if an opportunity looks pleasing on the outside, but doesn't line up with the plan You have for my life, lock the door and hide the key. I only want doors to be opened that You have ordained. And I know that You have great ones out there for me.

Help me to not manufacture things that I think are Your doors of opportunity. Give me wisdom to know whether or not an opportunity is of You. I know that You are not about confusion, but You are about perfect timing.

Scriptures

For a great door and effectual is opened unto me (1 Corinthians 16:9).

Trust in the Lord with all thine heart; and lean not unto thine own understanding. In all thy ways acknowledge him, and he shall direct thy paths (Proverbs 3:5,6).

He restoreth my soul: he leadeth me in the paths of righteousness for his name's sake (Psalm 23:3).

Divine Appointments and Connections

Holy Spirit, bring people across my path who can have a positive influence on my life. Order my steps to where I meet people who can help me in my purpose. Also, bring me across others' paths that I may help their purpose. It is so amazing how You have everything worked out. Thank You for always knowing the best routes, and for taking me there.

God, give me favor with people so that I may advance Your kingdom. I want to give You glory in everything. Give me a good name and favor with people. Thank You for knowing the people I am supposed to be in contact with.

Lord, I know that You want to bless me and put me in situations that are right for me, so I place it all in Your hands. Thanks for already speaking to the people I am supposed to meet and orchestrating our encounter. You are God. I don't even worry myself about Your plans because I know that You know what is best.

Scriptures

The steps of a good man are ordered by the Lord: and he delighteth in his way (Psalm 37:23).

A good name is rather to be chosen than great riches, and loving favour rather than silver and gold (Proverbs 22:1).

As for God, his way is perfect; the word of the Lord is tried: he is a buckler to all them that trust in him (2 Samuel 22:31).

When God's Call Seems Distant and Impossible

Jesus, sometimes I don't feel like I can do all that You have called me to do. The load seems to be too much for me to carry. But help me to not rely on feelings, but rather on what Your Word says. Your Word says that I am more than a conqueror and that I can do all things through You who give me strength. I know Your Word, but sometimes I feel so unworthy of Your call. I just ask that You will help me to know that even though I don't deserve all that You have done for me, through Your sacrifice I have been given Your authority, which is the greatest authority in heaven and on earth.

At times, the enemy tells me that You can't work through me until I'm in my twenties or thirties. But I know that You have told me to not let anyone look down on me because I am young, but to be an example. Help me to be an example, even when I feel unworthy. In myself, I am not worthy. And, in myself, the load is impossible to carry. But with You all things are possible.

Scriptures

Nay, in all these things we are more than conquerors through him that loved us (Romans 8:37).

I can do all things through Christ which strengtheneth me (Philippians 4:13).

Let no man despise thy youth; but be thou an example of the believers, in word, in conversation, in charity, in spirit, in faith, in purity (1 Timothy 4:12).

Recognizing Distractions

Father God, help me to keep my eyes fixed on the calling that You have for me. Without you, I know that I would fall away. But in You, I have the strength to stand against the enemy. Help me to not listen to the voices that tell me that I'm not worth anything, because I know that I am incredibly precious to You. Help me to not listen to the voices that say that Your way is not the right way, because I know who You are. Everything about You is right!

I don't want to do anything or go anywhere that is not pleasing to You. You are the greatest thing that has ever happened to me. Keep me away from counterfeits. I will never trade the promise that I have found in You for something else. You have my heart, Lord.

I will continue to read Your words and hide them in my heart. Through Your words I learn more about You, and the more I know about You, the more I want to stay on track with what You have for me.

Scriptures

I press toward the mark for the prize of the high calling of God in Christ Jesus (Philippians 3:14).

And this I speak for your own profit; not that I may cast a snare upon you, but for that which is comely, and that ye may attend upon the Lord without distraction (1 Corinthians 7:35).

But the word is very nigh unto thee, in thy mouth, and in thy heart, that thou mayest do it (Deuteronomy 30:14).

Making Plans

Holy Spirit, as I get ready to make important decisions, please tell me what You want me to do. I don't want them to be my plans. I want them to be Yours. Your plans are always the best. I don't want to make decisions based on what my friends are doing or what seems good on the outside. I want to know where You want me to go. However, I know that You may not tell me what You want me to do right away. Help me to be patient. I don't just seek answers, Lord. I seek You. You are the ultimate answer. You are the final answer.

Give my parents peace about what You want them to do. Thank You for giving them to me to help me make difficult decisions. Give them wisdom about the decisions we are to make together. Please eliminate stress from the decisions. I place it all in Your able hands. I give you the final say in every decision that I make, big or small.

Scriptures

A man's heart deviseth his way: but the Lord directeth his steps (Proverbs 16:9).

Trust in the Lord with all thine heart; and lean not unto thine own understanding. In all thy ways acknowledge him, and he shall direct thy paths (Proverbs 3:5,6).

If any of you lack wisdom, let him ask of God, that giveth to all men liberally, and upbraideth not; and it shall be given him (James 1:5).

Uncertain Future

Lord, I don't know what is ahead of me. My surroundings are beginning to change. The people in my life are beginning to change. Help me to not be afraid, and to always know that You are with me. You will only lead me in things that are good for me.

Thanks for being my Dad. Thanks for knowing what is best for me and for taking me there. Thanks for always leading me beside Your still waters and for holding me when I am scared. You are such an awesome God.

When deciding whether to go to college or to work, what school or what job to go to, how to pay for my future, or where I should live, I pray that You give me peace. Whisper in my ear what I should do.

I don't know where I should go, but You do and You will take me there. I don't know what I should do, but You do and You will show me how. I trust You because where my knowledge is limited, Yours is extraordinary. I love You, Jesus.

Scriptures

The Lord is my shepherd; I shall not want. He maketh me to lie down in green pastures: he leadeth me beside the still waters (Psalm 23:1,2).

Teach me to do thy will; for thou art my God: thy spirit is good; lead me into the land of uprightness (Psalm 143:10).

But as it is written, Eye hath not seen, nor ear heard, neither have entered into the heart of man, the things which God hath prepared for them that love him (1 Corinthians 2:9).

Facing the Future

Lord, the road ahead looks rough for me. I don't know where to go or what to do. Give me the strength to face what lies ahead head-on, and not fall short of the mark of the prize of the calling that You have for me. Help me to not be a coward, but to rely on the courage and confidence found in You.

You are the author of my future. If You are for me, then who can be against me? Why should I worry about the future when You *are* my future? I make a commitment to put my foundation in You. You are the source of my strength.

Hold my hand as I dive into the future. Guide me in all Your truth. Remind me of what Your Word says, so that I can know who I am in You. Even though I may not completely know what lies ahead, thank You for not giving me a spirit of fear, but of power, love, and a sound mind. I put my hope in You. Thank You, Jesus.

Scriptures

What shall we then say to these things? If God be for us, who can be against us? (Romans 8:31).

I press toward the mark for the prize of the high calling of God in Christ Jesus (Philippians 3:14).

For God hath not given us the spirit of fear; but of power, and of love, and of a sound mind (2 Timothy 1:7).

III

My Spiritual Growth

Help From the Holy Spirit

Father God, I thank You for the gift of the Holy Spirit that You have given to me. I thank You that He is my comforter and counselor, my helper and intercessor. Holy Spirit, You are my advocate, my strengthener, and my partner in my walk of faith. You teach me all things. You will remind me of the truths from Your Word.

Holy Spirit, I invite You into every part of my life. Show me God's ways. Help me to know my Father's will and to carry His love into my world today.

Give me wisdom concerning every decision that I need to make. Anoint me so I can do my schoolwork and my extracurricular activities with excellence. Give me the strength and courage to do Your will and to be obedient to Your voice today. Strengthen my body so I have the physical stamina, endurance, and strength to do all that is required of me.

Let the light of Your love shine brightly through me. Holy Spirit, be real to my friends through me today. Help me to apply the truth and principles of God's Word to every area of my life.

Scriptures

And I will pray the Father, and he shall give you another Comforter, that he may abide with you for ever (John 14:16).

But the Comforter, which is the Holy Ghost, whom the Father will send in my name, he shall teach you all things, and bring all things to your remembrance, whatsoever I have said unto you (John 14:26).

But if the Spirit of him that raised up Jesus from the dead dwell in you, he that raised up Christ from the dead shall also quicken your mortal bodies by his Spirit that dwelleth in you (Romans 8:11).

My Hope in God

Father God, in Jesus' name, I thank You that when I accepted the Lord Jesus as my personal Savior, Jesus Himself came to live in my heart. The Holy Spirit came to make His home in me. My life has been redeemed from destruction. My sins have been forgiven. I have been washed clean by the blood of my Lord and Savior, Jesus. My heart is new. Old things are passed way. I became new in Christ.

When I sin, Jesus represents my case to You, Father. When I ask for forgiveness, You are faithful and just to forgive me of my sins. When I need direction, the Holy Spirit is there to help me find my way. Your Word, Lord, is a lamp and a light in my life. Your Word is my standard to live by; it helps me lead a life that pleases You.

I have a new destiny, a new hope, a new joy, and a new purpose. My eternal home is with my Lord and Savior. I will be with You and all the saints in heaven forever. For eternity, I will praise Your name and enjoy Your presence.

Scriptures

Therefore if any man be in Christ, he is a new creature: old things are passed away; behold, all things are become new (2 Corinthians 5:17).

My little children, these things write I unto you, that ye sin not. And if any man sin, we have an advocate with the Father, Jesus Christ the righteous (1 John 2:1).

Thy word is a lamp unto my feet, and a light unto my path (Psalm 119:105).

How to Pray

Father, You said that I should tell You what I need. You said to come boldly to Your throne room to receive grace and mercy. Your Word says that when I pray in belief, I have whatever I pray for. I want to learn to pray.

Help me to not get so busy that I give up the joy and power of spending time with You in prayer. Put a desire in my heart to pray more and to make prayer a big part of my life. Help me to schedule certain times of the day to pray and seek Your wisdom. Help me to not be distracted during my prayer time, but to be able to focus on You and Your Word.

Use me to pray for others. Help me to be sensitive to the voice of the Holy Spirit. Help me to be quick to obey the call to prayer whenever I sense Your direction to pray. Let prayer become so significant to me that it becomes my natural response to everything that happens in my life.

Your Word says that the passionate prayers of the righteous avail much. Show me how to pray passionately and effectively.

Scriptures

Be careful for nothing; but in every thing by prayer and supplication with thanksgiving let your requests be made known unto God (Philippians 4:6).

Let us therefore come boldly unto the throne of grace, that we may obtain mercy, and find grace to help in time of need (Hebrews 4:16).

Therefore I say unto you, What things soever ye desire, when ye pray, believe that ye receive them, and ye shall have them (Mark 11:24).

Likewise the Spirit also helpeth our infirmities: for we know not what we should pray for as we ought: but the Spirit itself maketh intercession for us with groanings which cannot be uttered (Romans 8:26).

The effectual fervent prayer of a righteous man availeth much (James 5:16).

Hunger for God

Lord, in Jesus' name I pray that You would create a deeper hunger in my heart for You. Bring back the desire, passion, and thirst for You that I had when I first became a Christian. Lord, I love You, but I want to have a hunger for You. Help me to fall in love with You again. Let my main goal in life be to know You and the depths of Your love and compassion.

Show me who You are; reveal Your character to me. Help me to become passionately and deeply acquainted with You. I crave Your presence in and on my life throughout the day. I want to know You better.

Help me to be sensitive to the voice of Your Spirit. Let me see with Your eyes and hear with Your ears. Let me carry Your love and compassion to the world.

I pray, Lord, that Your presence will become such an intimate part of my life that others will see You in every part of my character. Fill my life to overflowing with Your presence. I pray that knowing You intimately will become the greatest quest of my life.

Scriptures

As the hart panteth after the water brooks, so panteth my soul after thee, O God (Psalm 42:1).

That Christ may dwell in your hearts by faith; that ye, being rooted and grounded in love, may be able to comprehend with all saints what is the breadth, and length, and depth, and height (Ephesians 3:17,18).

And be not drunk with wine, wherein is excess; but be filled with the Spirit (Ephesians 5:18).

Putting God and His Word First

Dear Father, I am going to put You and Your Word first in my life. I make Your Word the authority, the standard, and the final word to live my life by. I seek Your Word as counsel for every area of my life. I am quick to obey the instructions from Your Word.

The Bible is Your Word to me. It is alive, powerful, and the source of wisdom, instruction, and direction for my life. Lord, show me the truths and principles of Your Word. Speak to me through its wisdom and instruction.

Help me to take time to study Your Word and apply its principles to my life. Help me to find creative ways to memorize Scripture and to learn more of Your Word. As I read Your Word, speak to me. Correct me, direct me, guide me, and show me what You want me to do. Give me wisdom through Your Word to always bring You honor with my life.

Scriptures

This book of the law shall not depart out of thy mouth; but thou shalt meditate therein day and night, that thou mayest observe to do according to all that is written therein: for then thou shalt make thy way prosperous, and then thou shalt have good success (Joshua 1:8).

But his delight is in the law of the Lord; and in his law doth he meditate day and night (Psalm 1:2).

Keep therefore the words of this covenant, and do them, that ye may prosper in all that ye do (Deuteronomy 28:9).

Walking in the Fullness of God's Plan

Lord, in all my ways I recognize, acknowledge, and honor You. I put You first in my life. I lean on You, trust in You, and am confident in You, Lord. With all my heart and mind I rely on You. Give me Your insight and understanding about every part of my life. Thank You, Lord, for blessing me and favoring me in the sight of other people. Because I acknowledge You, You direct, make straight, and regulate all my ways. My steps are sure, and my path is clear. My future is bright and promising.

You are my promise of a future crowned with Your blessing. Fulfill Your plans and purposes for my life. Use me, Lord, to make a difference in this world. Develop in me a heart of a champion. Give me courage and the spirit of a warrior.

Let my life be a testimony of Your grace, love, and mercy. Let me be so full of You that there is none of me left.

Consume my life, Lord, to the point that others only see You in me.

Scriptures

In all thy ways acknowledge him, and he shall direct thy paths (Proverbs 3:6).

By so much was Jesus made a surety of a better testament (Hebrews 7:22).

He must increase, but I must decrease (John 3:30).

IV

When I Need...

Confidence

Lord, at times I rely on my own strength, and I get scared that I can't do what I'm supposed to do. I usually do one of two things: I either become completely insecure and stay away from anything that I could possibly fail at, or I try to mask my insecurity with a false confidence; that's when I get cocky. Lord, I don't want to be insecure anymore, because I know that You see me as valuable, and what You think is all that matters. Thanks for thinking that I am special. Thanks for calling me Your child. Help me to know that in You, I can stand against anything. Your Word says that if I am supposed to, I could say "move" to the mountain and it would move. How cool is that? You are such an awesome God! I found everything in life solely in You, God. Thank You for Your confidence.

Help me to reach out in confidence to others who are down. Give me the strength to tell them about the confidence that is found in Your love. I want my light of Your love to shine.

Scriptures

I will praise thee; for I am fearfully and wonderfully made: marvellous are thy works; and that my soul knoweth right well (Psalm 139:14).

For verily I say unto you, That whosoever shall say unto this mountain, Be thou removed, and be thou cast into the sea; and shall not doubt in his heart, but shall believe that those things which he saith shall come to pass; he shall have whatsoever he saith (Mark 11:23).

Then he answered and spake unto me, saying, This is the word of the Lord unto Zerubbabel, saying, Not by might, nor by power, but by my spirit, saith the Lord of hosts (Zechariah 4:6).

Courage

Lord, give me the strength to be able to step out of my comfort zone when You call me to. Help me to not always rely on situations and people that are familiar, but to step out and take risks that are needed. But, Lord, I make a decision to always seek You in what risks to take and to not take. I always want to be under Your almighty hand.

Help me to not be afraid of failure, because You can always work things together for my good because I am your child and I have a special purpose that You have designed. Thank You, Lord, that You love me even if I fail.

Give me a boldness that can only come from You. I don't want it to be a boldness in myself, but in You who live inside of me. Lord, just as You gave Joshua strength to lead Your people into the land that You promised them, please give me strength to go to the places that You have for me without fear or doubt. You are such a great God.

Scriptures

And we know that all things work together for good to them that love God, to them who are the called according to his purpose (Romans 8:28).

The Lord will fulfill his purpose for me; your love, O Lord, endures forever... (Psalm 138:8).

Be strong and of a good courage, fear not, nor be afraid of them: for the Lord thy God, he it is that doth go with thee; he will not fail thee, nor forsake thee (Deuteronomy 31:6).

Deliverance From Substance Addictions

God, You know that the enemy has thrown a counterfeit at me, but You can restore all things back to me. I need Your strength because I can't make it on my own. Be my guide. Help me to realize that I don't need this to be happy. All I need is You. Lord, thank You that You don't just bring happiness, but You bring joy. Joy is happiness through any circumstances. Even when things are looking down, You are my joy. You are not a high that runs out. You are everlasting.

Deliver me from this addiction. I know that it may take time, and I am willing to work. Bring people across my path who can help me make it through. I need You. Help me to be open about my addiction because I know that I am not alone. You care about me, and so do Your people. Thank You for loving me through this and for calling me Your child. Stand by me. People may say bad things about me, but I don't care! You love me. That's all that is important.

Scriptures

He brought me forth also into a large place; he delivered me, because he delighted in me (Psalm 18:19).

But God, who is rich in mercy, for his great love wherewith he loved us (Ephesians 2:4).

And it shall come to pass, that in the place where it was said unto them, Ye are not my people; there shall they be called the children of the living God (Romans 9:26).

Encouragement

God, I am on my face before You. With all that has happened, You are still my God. Thanks for being good all the time. Even when the road seems confusing, You are right there with me.

Lord, even in the dark, I reach out and grab hold of You. Lead me, Lord. Walk with me through the storm, and help me to see the light on the other side. Even in my trials, You are there. Even when no one else is there, You are. Even when I mess up, You are there for me, Jesus. I love You so much.

I trade in all of the stress of the difficult things in my life for Your unfailing love that nudges me on. Thanks for picking me up out of my distress. Thanks for Your joy, Lord. Your life is so awesome! Your life keeps me going. When the world crumbles around me, You surround me, Lord! Thank You so much. Keep me up, Lord. Even though storms may come, be the lifter of my head.

Scriptures

But I trust in your unfailing love; my heart rejoices in your salvation (Psalm 13:5).

In my distress I called upon the Lord, and cried unto my God: he heard my voice out of his temple, and my cry came before him, even into his ears.... He sent from above, he took me, he drew me out of many waters (Psalm 18:6,16).

But thou, O Lord, art a shield for me; my glory, and the lifter up of mine head (Psalm 3:3).

Faith

Lord, thank You for giving me a measure of faith. You are the author and finisher of my faith. You mature and perfect the faith that You have placed within my heart.

You said that faith comes by hearing the Word of God. Lord, I will read and meditate on Your Word every day, and as I do faith will grow in my heart. You said that without faith it is impossible to please You. I want to please You: Help me to have strong faith. Faith is the assurance and confirmation, my title deed, of things that I hope for and the proof of things I do not see. Lord, thank You that the faith that is in my heart perceives the unseen promise as a real fact.

I am not moved by what I see but only by what I believe, and I believe You. By faith, I bring into my life every promise from Your Word. Regardless of what happens around me, Lord, I say that Your promises are "yes and amen." Faith is alive and working in my life, and by faith I receive everything You have done for me, in Jesus' name.

Praise Be to God.
Amen

Scriptures

...God hath dealt to every man the measure of faith (Romans 12:3).

Looking unto Jesus the author and finisher of our faith; who for the joy that was set before him endured the cross, despising the shame, and is set down at the right hand of the throne of God (Hebrews 12:2).

So then faith cometh by hearing, and hearing by the word of God (Romans 10:17).

But without faith it is impossible to please him: for he that cometh to God must believe that he is, and that he is a rewarder of them that diligently seek him (Hebrews 11:6).

Now faith is the substance of things hoped for, the evidence of things not seen (Hebrews 11:1).

For all the promises of God in him are yea, and in him Amen, unto the glory of God by us (2 Corinthians 1:20).

Favor

God, I ask that You would give me favor with other people. Help them to see You inside of me. I don't want favor because they see what I do or my accomplishments, but because they see Your genuineness inside of me. Jesus, just as You grew in favor with people, help me to also grow in that favor.

Lord, help me to use this favor only to further Your kingdom, not for my own benefit. Everywhere that I go, I want people to see You. When people see You in my life, they will want to show me favor. Thank You for placing Your Spirit inside of me, so that others can see.

Thank You for Your love and peace in my life. I want nothing more than to honor You. Thank You that when I use Your name, You are working. Thank You that Your name turns heads. Thank You for the favor that You have given me with others. Help me to use that favor to honor and serve You. I give You all of the glory, Jesus.

Scriptures

And Jesus increased in wisdom and stature, and in favour with God and man (Luke 2:52).

For thou, Lord, wilt bless the righteous; with favour wilt thou compass him as with a shield (Psalm 5:12).

So shalt thou find favour and good understanding in the sight of God and man (Proverbs 3:4).

Guidance

Lord Jesus, thanks for revealing to me through Your Word the secret of facing every situation. I know what to do when I find myself in difficult circumstances, and I know what to do when everything is going well: I thank You, Lord, that I have learned that in every circumstance You are my strength, my salvation, and my deliverer.

The power of Your Word in my life can take care of me in every situation. I can do all things through Your power that is within me. Because of Your anointing and the power of Your Word, not a single circumstance can hold me down or stop me from living a life of victory. I am self-sufficient in Your sufficiency.

I thank You, Lord, that by the wisdom of Your Word and the guidance of Your Spirit I can navigate my way through any circumstance. Help me, Lord, to hear Your voice clearly and distinctly. Help me to be sensitive to the guidance of the Holy Spirit. Lord, let me rely completely on You and not on my own understanding.

Scriptures

I know what it is to be in need, and I know what it is to have plenty. I have learned the secret of being content in any and every situation, whether well fed or hungry, whether living in plenty or in want (Philippians 4:12).

I can do all things through Christ which strengtheneth me (Philippians 4:13).

Trust in the Lord with all thine heart; and lean not unto thine own understanding (Proverbs 3:5).

Loving Myself as God Loves Me

Heavenly Father, I ask that You help me to love myself. Help me to see myself the way You see me, as a valuable gift for whose redemption You gave the life of Your own Son. Help me to realize that You have placed within me unique qualities, talents, and gifts. Help me to appreciate what You have done for me.

Help me to see with Your eyes, not with my eyes or others' eyes. Help me to recognize that I am a work in progress and that, even though I am not what I want to be, I am not what I used to be. I am growing in You and am beautiful in Your sight.

Give me confidence to love myself the way You love me. Help me to not be critical or condemning of myself but to encourage myself in You. Help me to be quick to forgive myself when I make mistakes and quick to encourage myself. Help me to realize that, even with all my shortcomings, You love me and believe in me. Help me to do the same for myself.

I recognize that it is Your will that I let Your light and love shine through me to my wife, children, coworkers, friends, and all those I meet. I also realize that if I do not love myself, then it is hard for me to love others. Help me to not listen to the voice of the enemy or to the voice of others, but to listen to Your voice. Your Word says that I am unique, that I am a special gift, that I am a treasure in Your sight. I choose to believe You and to order my life by that. Give me confidence and faith to love myself, in Jesus' name.

Scriptures

But God, who is rich in mercy, for his great love wherewith he loved us, even when we were dead in sins, hath quickened us together with Christ, (by grace ye are saved;) and hath raised us up together, and made us sit together in heavenly places in Christ Jesus (Ephesians 2:4-6).

Wherefore comfort yourselves together, and edify one another, even as also ye do (1 Thessalonians 5:11).

I will praise thee; for I am fearfully and wonderfully made: marvellous are thy works; and that my soul knoweth right well (Psalm 139:14).

New Ideas

Jesus, give me new inspiration for what is to come. Show me the best ways for using the gifts and abilities that You have given to me. I don't want my ideas to be from anyone but You, because Your ideas are always the best ones. I dedicate myself to spending time with You so that You can share these ideas with me and prepare me for the day.

You are the most creative person that I have ever met. Everything that You think of is amazing! I can tell this just through Your creation. Everywhere I look, I see a new reflection of You. I know that You want to share Your creativity with me. I want to open myself up to that. Help me to distinguish the ideas that come from You from the ideas that come from other places. I want You to be my sole source for ideas. I will not look to outside sources, but to You because You are such an amazing God who knows what is right for me. I love You.

Scriptures

How precious also are thy thoughts unto me, O God! how great is the sum of them! (Psalm 139:17).

For the invisible things of him from the creation of the world are clearly seen, being understood by the things that are made, even his eternal power and Godhead; so that they are without excuse (Romans 1:20).

Shew me thy ways, O Lord; teach me thy paths (Psalm 25:4).

Peace

Lord, thank You that when I am confused, You are there. When my emotions are telling me one thing and my mind is telling me something else, You can come in with the answer of what to do. Even if Your response is not always instantaneous, You are there. I know that You are always there. Even in the times when I think that my circumstances are not important to You, they always are.

Lord, in the night when I lie down to sleep, that time is the hardest. Thank You for being there when I feel alone. Thank You that even when what I'm worrying about is not that big of a deal to other people, it is big to You. You care about me. I can't tell You how much that means to me.

Give me sweet sleep. I don't want to worry any more. I want to give it all over to You. You already know the outcome, and You've worked it for my good. You've brought me through so much so far in my life. You're always faithful.

Scriptures

Are not five sparrows sold for two farthings, and not one of them is forgotten before God? But even the very hairs of your head are all numbered. Fear not therefore: ye are of more value than many sparrows (Luke 12:6,7).

It is vain for you to rise up early, to sit up late, to eat the bread of sorrows: for so he giveth his beloved sleep (Psalm 127:2).

Casting all your care upon him; for he careth for you (1 Peter 5:7).

Receiving Forgiveness

Lord, thank You for Your forgiveness. Thank You for Your love that looks past all that I've done and restores me back to You. Thank You, Lord, that You have seen my ways but You will heal me. You will guide me and restore comfort to me. Thank You, Lord, that no matter what I have done You will always love me and restore me.

I find comfort in Your promise that You will never leave me or forsake me. Thank You that neither height nor depth, angels nor demons, present nor future, nor anything else in creation could separate me from Your love. Thank You that You can give back anything that the enemy has taken from me.

I cannot fix what is broken. Only You can. Thanks for taking what is broken in me and molding it into something awesome, ready to be used by You. I love You so much because You first loved me. Thanks for the peace that I find in Your restoration. You are such an amazing God.

Scriptures

I have seen his ways, and will heal him: I will lead him also, and restore comforts unto him and to his mourners (Isaiah 57:18).

Let your conversation be without covetousness; and be content with such things as ye have: for he hath said, I will never leave thee, nor forsake thee (Hebrews 13:5).

For I am persuaded, that neither death, nor life, nor angels, nor principalities, nor powers, nor things present, nor things to come, nor height, nor depth, nor any other creature, shall be able to separate us from the love of God, which is in Christ Jesus our Lord (Romans 8:38,39).

Resurrection Power

Lord, in Jesus' name, I thank You that I am not controlled by my body's desires or the desires of my old nature. The old nature is gone, and I am a completely new person. The same Spirit that raised my Lord Jesus from the dead lives in me. The same resurrection power gives life, health, and vitality to my body. By that same resurrection power, I live a winning life and not a losing one. Your Word is in my heart, and I accomplish great things in Your name.

Your resurrection power in me renews my mind and strengthens my spirit. By Your power in me, Lord, I can do all things. That power gives me boldness and confidence to be a witness for You. Your power is working in me, changing me into Your image, developing in me Your nature.

By the same resurrection power, my life has taken on a new dimension—a dimension of winning faith, spiritual endurance, and total victory in every area of my life.

Scriptures

Therefore if any man be in Christ, he is a new creature: old things are passed away; behold, all things are become new (2 Corinthians 5:17).

But if the Spirit of him that raised up Jesus from the dead dwell in you, he that raised up Christ from the dead shall also quicken your mortal bodies by his Spirit that dwelleth in you (Romans 8:11).

I can do all things through Christ which strengtheneth me (Philippians 4:13).

For if we have been planted together in the likeness of his death, we shall be also in the likeness of his resurrection (Romans 6:5).

Safety and Protection

Keep me safe, Lord. Watch over me, and don't let anything interfere with my life or my purpose. Help me to see bad situations and how to avoid them. Thank You that Your favor surrounds me like a shield and that I don't have to worry because Your hand is my shelter. I want to hide in the shadow of Your wings. There is nowhere that I could go to escape Your presence, Lord. Even if my whole world falls, I can rest in You. Though thousands may fall at my side, and even more may fall at the other side, You won't allow me to fall.

Shelter me with Your mercy. Thanks for meeting me in our secret place, and thank You that I can find that place wherever I go. All I have to do is call on Your name. You are such a great God, and You are so faithful to walk with me to protect me. I won't leave Your side, Lord.

Scriptures

For thou, Lord, wilt bless the righteous; with favour wilt thou compass him as with a shield (Psalm 5:12).

Whither shall I go from thy spirit? or whither shall I flee from thy presence? .... Even there shall thy hand lead me, and thy right hand shall hold me (Psalm 139:7,10).

A thousand shall fall at thy side, and ten thousand at thy right hand; but it shall not come nigh thee (Psalm 91:7).

Strength for Battle

Father God, in Jesus' name, I ask You to help me to not become weary in well doing. Help me to not be complacent or apathetic, but to be willing and obedient to fight spiritual battles when You need me to.

I am strong in You. I am empowered through my union with You. I draw strength from You for every battle that I face in life. I put on the whole armor today. I put myself in a position to successfully stand against all the attacks of Satan and the forces of darkness.

This battle I am fighting is not with humans. No human being is my enemy. I will not direct my attack toward any person. My enemies are Satan and his demonic forces.

Because of Your armor, Lord, I am able to resist the enemy, stand my ground, and win in the day of conflict and danger. When crisis comes to my life, I am bold to fight, to proclaim Your Word, and to stand upon Your promises. I firmly stand my ground and, having done all that the crisis may demand, I stand strong and hold my ground in the middle of the battle, knowing that ultimate victory is certain in You!

Scriptures

And let us not be weary in well doing: for in due season we shall reap, if we faint not (Galatians 6:9).

For we wrestle not against flesh and blood, but against principalities, against powers, against the rulers of the darkness of this world, against spiritual wickedness in high places (Ephesians 6:12).

Wherefore take unto you the whole armour of God, that ye may be able to withstand in the evil day, and having done all, to stand (Ephesians 6:13).

Wisdom

God, before all else, I ask You for wisdom. I know that when Solomon asked for wisdom, everything else followed. I don't ask for selfish gain. I ask so that I might know You more and follow Your ways to a greater extent. I know that ultimate wisdom comes from You alone. Give me not just knowledge, but You. Fearing You is the beginning of knowledge. I know that this fear doesn't mean being afraid. It means giving You the honor and respect that You deserve. I give You all of the honor, glory, and power, Lord. You are so great.

I want to use wisdom to further Your kingdom, Lord. I want others to see You through my life. Every day I wake up, teach me more about who You are so that I can tell the world. Help me share with my friends about the wisdom that You have given me. I want so badly for them to see You. I know that their lives will change radically once they catch a glimpse of You. You are a radical, life-changing God. Thank You for changing my life with Your love and wisdom.

Scriptures

And God said to Solomon, Because this was in thine heart, and thou hast not asked riches, wealth, or honour, nor the life of thine enemies, neither yet hast asked long life; but hast asked wisdom and knowledge for thyself, that thou mayest judge my people, over whom I have made thee king: Wisdom and knowledge is granted unto thee; and I will give thee riches, and wealth, and honour, such as none of the kings have had that have been before thee, neither shall there any after thee have the like (2 Chronicles 1:11,12).

The fear of the Lord is the beginning of knowledge: but fools despise wisdom and instruction (Proverbs 1:7).

If any of you lack wisdom, let him ask of God, that giveth to all men liberally, and upbraideth not; and it shall be given him (James 1:5).

V

When I Face...

A Crisis

Jesus, help me to realize that crisis is normal in life. I don't want to be afraid, nervous, or overwhelmed when I find myself in a crisis situation. Help me to not react in confusion, worry, or desperation.

You said that in this world we would have tribulation but to be of good cheer because You have overcome the world. Help me to keep a good attitude and a cheerful heart no matter what I'm facing.

You said that life would get tough sometimes, even for the people who trust You, but that You would deliver us every time. Deliver me out of this crisis; show me how You will make everything right again. Help me to keep my mind on You and the power of Your Word. Give me wisdom and show me what to do.

I count it all joy when I am faced with trials and testing, knowing that the trying of my faith builds my patience and godly character. You have promised to deliver me, and I know You will. Give me courage and strength to not give up or give in but to patiently keep trusting You until my deliverance comes.

Scriptures

These things I have spoken unto you, that in me ye might have peace. In the world ye shall have tribulation: but be of good cheer; I have overcome the world (John 16:33).

Many are the afflictions of the righteous: but the Lord delivereth him out of them all (Psalm 34:19).

My brethren, count it all joy when ye fall into divers temptations; knowing this, that the trying of your faith worketh patience. But let patience have her perfect work, that ye may be perfect and entire, wanting nothing (James 1:2-4).

Discouragement

I know that overcoming is a choice. And I make that choice, but sometimes my discouragement becomes so great that I need Your supernatural strength to make that decision. Help me to not base who I am on my superficial accomplishments. I place my worth totally and completely in You. I am totally loved, accepted, and identified in You. This is a love not determined by what I've done.

So there is no need for discouragement because of what seems to be failures. You love me anyway, and that's all that is important. I make the decision to overcome when the enemy tries to hold me down. Nothing will hold me down. On the contrary, You will lift me up. Thank You so much! When I fell down, You picked me up and brushed off the dust that was on me. Thank You, Jesus.

Thank You for the journey of life, Lord. Thank You for walking with me. Through the cross, You have turned my mourning into dancing. I throw off my discouragement and seek You.

Scriptures

But God, who is rich in mercy, for his great love wherewith he loved us, even when we were dead in sins, hath quickened us together with Christ, (by grace ye are saved) (Ephesians 2:4,5).

Not by works of righteousness which we have done, but according to his mercy he saved us, by the washing of regeneration, and renewing of the Holy Ghost (Titus 3:5).

Thou hast turned for me my mourning into dancing: thou hast put off my sackcloth, and girded me with gladness (Psalm 30:11).

An Exam

Jesus, I find peace in You as I take this exam. I am nervous, and I need Your help to remember the answers. Holy Spirit, bring back to my remembrance all that I have studied. And if I haven't studied enough, bring back all of the lectures, homework, or anything else that I have done in this class. Give me the mind of Christ. You know everything, including all of the answers to this test. I give You this test, and ask that in Your wisdom You would whisper the answers in my ear.

Lord, give me the strength to not cheat. I would never want to do something that is against Your character. Also, help me to know how much to study before each exam. I know that You reward all of the work that I have put in. You know that my desire is to do well in school. Give me practical steps to be able to accomplish that goal.

I also pray for the other members of my class. Give us all peace and the ability to do well on this test. Thank You, Holy Spirit.

Scriptures

But the Comforter, which is the Holy Ghost, whom the Father will send in my name, he shall teach you all things, and bring all things to your remembrance, whatsoever I have said unto you (John 14:26).

For who hath known the mind of the Lord, that he may instruct him? but we have the mind of Christ (1 Corinthians 2:16).

Study to shew thyself approved unto God, a workman that needeth to not be ashamed, rightly dividing the word of truth (2 Timothy 2:15).

Fatigue

Lord, I ask You for strength in my body. Restore to me energy and vitality to go on. Lord, I understand that mental frustrations and worries can make me tired, so I give you every care in my life. Please strengthen my spirit, soul, and body today. I draw from Your encouragement and the power of Your Word. Just as David did, I encourage myself in You, Lord. You are my strength.

Thank You for Your peace and rest. Help me to rest and do what is right for my body. I know my body is the temple of Your Spirit. Help me to properly rest, exercise, and eat so I am not fighting against my body but helping to keep my body strong. Thank You for renewing Your strength within me.

Help me, Lord, to not become weak, weary, or faint as I do Your will but to gain strength through my union with You, so I can accomplish all that You have called me to do. Help me to not become tired, overworked, or stressed but to let Your joy fill my heart and strengthen my body.

Scriptures

Cast thy burden upon the Lord, and he shall sustain thee: he shall never suffer the righteous to be moved (Psalm 55:22).

What? know ye not that your body is the temple of the Holy Ghost which is in you, which ye have of God, and ye are not your own? (1 Corinthians 6:19).

And let us not be weary in well doing: for in due season we shall reap, if we faint not (Galatians 6:9).

Fear

Lord, thank You for Your power. Thank You for the strength to conquer fear. When I'm afraid, I know that I can call upon Your name. Thank You that You have not given me a spirit of fear, but of power, love, and a sound mind. I'm not afraid when I have You, because You created all things and You have given me dominion over all things through Your Son, Jesus.

Your name is so powerful. Nothing can stand against the name of Jesus. I'm sorry that I may doubt Your power at times. Remind me that You have me under Your wings. Under Your wings I am filled with love and power. I can't go anywhere to escape Your love, even though I may try. And it is Your love that casts out all fear. Renew my mind with Your love every day. Help me to know even more of the power that You possess. I am weak, but when I let You work through me I am strong. Thank You for Your power.

Scriptures

For God hath not given us the spirit of fear; but of power, and of love, and of a sound mind (2 Timothy 1:7).

And he said unto me, My grace is sufficient for thee: for my strength is made perfect in weakness. Most gladly therefore will I rather glory in my infirmities, that the power of Christ may rest upon me (2 Corinthians 12:9).

Whither shall I go from thy spirit? or whither shall I flee from thy presence? .... Even there shall thy hand lead me, and thy right hand shall hold me (Psalm 139:7,10).

Grief

I'm hurting, Lord. I need Your comfort. With everything that I have inside of me, I cry out for Your love. Comfort me, Holy Spirit. Help me through this grieving process. This is the worst feeling in the world, and I know that nothing else will help me now. I feel like a part of me is gone. I've tried to make it seem like I am okay, but I am not. I am crying out for someone to fix what has been broken in my heart. You, Lord, can make me whole again. You, Jesus, can see through the facade, past my emotions, to my heart. And You can show Your love to me in a way that I've never seen before.

I know that this grief is a process. I'm not asking that You take this away. I'm just asking that You stay with me through the pain. I'm asking that You would hold me in Your arms and whisper to me how much You love me. Lord, thank You for the memories and for the promise that I will see them again someday.

Scriptures

But the Comforter, which is the Holy Ghost, whom the Father will send in my name, he shall teach you all things, and bring all things to your remembrance, whatsoever I have said unto you (John 14:26).

This is my comfort in my affliction: for thy word hath quickened me (Psalm 119:50).

Trust in him at all times, O people; pour out your hearts to him, for God is our refuge (Psalm 62:8).

Hard Times

Father, I thank You that even though at times I might be troubled and oppressed, I am never crushed.

Even though I sometimes may get embarrassed and be faced with tough situations, even though it seems as if I am unable to find my way out, I will never despair.

Even though I may be disliked, called names, and persecuted, I know You will never leave me or forsake me. You will never desert me to stand alone.

Even though I may be struck down to the ground, I will never be struck out or destroyed. I will never give in, give up, or quit. You are with me, You are for me, and You are in me—so I always win.

You said that in this world life might get tough but to be of good cheer because You have overcome this world. You said that the righteous would have many times when life would get hard but You would deliver us out of them all. Thank You, Lord, for delivering me.

Scriptures

We are troubled on every side, yet not distressed; we are perplexed, but not in despair; persecuted, but not forsaken; cast down, but not destroyed; always bearing about in the body the dying of the Lord Jesus, that the life also of Jesus might be made manifest in our body (2 Corinthians 4:8-10).

...for he hath said, I will never leave thee, nor forsake thee (Hebrews 13:5).

These things I have spoken unto you, that in me ye might have peace. In the world ye shall have tribulation: but be of good cheer; I have overcome the world (John 16:33).

Many are the afflictions of the righteous: but the Lord delivereth him out of them all (Psalm 34:19).

Peer Pressure

Father, since I have so much worth in Your eyes, I don't need to find worth in others' eyes. Continue to remind me of that. Resisting the pressure of my friends to do things that I know are not right can be very hard at times. Give me the strength to overcome it through Your love in my life.

Give me the ability to say no and to not follow the crowd. Help me to be a trendsetter and a world-changer rather than a follower. I know that You are my God and You want me to be in the world but not of it. Help me to catch that vision. I know that this world is not my home. Heaven is my home. Things of this world shouldn't sweep me away, because what I have waiting for me at home is so much better.

Lord, give me the words to say that will impact my friends' lives, but don't let me be sucked into their activities that do not glorify You. Help me to not worry about their making fun of me for my convictions, but help me stand for You always.

Scriptures

And be not conformed to this world: but be ye transformed by the renewing of your mind, that ye may prove what is that good, and acceptable, and perfect, will of God (Romans 12:2).

For all that is in the world, the lust of the flesh, and the lust of the eyes, and the pride of life, is not of the Father, but is of the world (1 John 2:16).

Now we have received, not the spirit of the world, but the spirit which is of God; that we might know the things that are freely given to us of God (1 Corinthians 2:12).

Rejection

Jesus, thank You for the cross. Thank You that through the cross, You accepted me just as I am. I don't need to rely on the opinions of others, because I know that You have a great opinion of me. God, You loved me so much that You sent Your only Son to die for me so that I could know how special I am to You.

Even though I know that You love me, it is still hard when others reject me. Help me to just continue to walk in love and not bitterness. Help me to view every person as an awesome creation and a unique reflection of You.

Lord, I thank You that I am made in Your image. Your Word says that I am fearfully and wonderfully made. I know that what You make is wonderful, Lord. And You made me. Even though I have messed up and am no longer worthy on my own, to You I am priceless. Thank You for viewing me as the apple of Your eye. I love You so much. You are awesome in everything that You do.

Scriptures

For God so loved the world, that he gave his only begotten Son, that whosoever believeth in him should not perish, but have everlasting life (John 3:16).

I will praise thee; for I am fearfully and wonderfully made: marvellous are thy works; and that my soul knoweth right well (Psalm 139:14).

All have sinned and fall short of the glory of God, and are justified freely by his grace through the redemption that came by Christ Jesus (Romans 3:23,24).

He shielded him and cared for him; he guarded him as the apple of his eye (Deuteronomy 32:10).

Someone Who Lies About Me

God, thank You that Your Word is the source of all truth. I make the commitment to not be bothered by what people say about me, because You know the truth and that is all that matters. Lord, help people to see my relationship with You and to not believe what someone else might say. Please convict this person who is telling the lies, and help (him/her) to come out with the truth.

It hurts when people tell lies about you. I know that You know that. People used to say all kinds of bad things about You. They even said that You were born of Satan! But I thank You for Your example. You were not shaken by what they said. You stood firm and did what God called You to do. You knew the truth. You were the truth! You *are* the truth! Thank You that since I know You, You (the truth) have set me free! Thank You for the freedom in knowing that it doesn't matter what others say. All that matters is the truth: You are all that matters, Jesus.

Scriptures

Sanctify them through thy truth: thy word is truth (John 17:17).

But I say unto you, That every idle word that men shall speak, they shall give account thereof in the day of judgment. For by thy words thou shalt be justified, and by thy words thou shalt be condemned (Matthew 12:36,37).

And ye shall know the truth, and the truth shall make you free (John 8:32).

Stressful Situations

Lord, why should I worry about what I will eat or what I will wear? These are all surface, earthly things. You have these things under control. Stress is so unnecessary. Why do I spend so much time worrying about these things when I can just give them to the Creator of the universe? Jesus, I rely on You for everything in my life. Help me through stress. I get so worried about things sometimes instead of relying on You. I don't want to do that anymore.

Since You have all power, and I have You, I have victory over everything that is not in Your will. I can have victory over stress. Thank You for that victory. Stress is not good for me. It can cause problems in my body and my mind. I want to stay away from stress. When I get concerned about something, help me to give it to You. That way, I will avoid stress.

Lord, thank You that You will give me wisdom on how to get out of bad situations. I give You all things that concern me and ask that Your will would be done in my life, Lord.

Scriptures

Therefore I say unto you, Take no thought for your life, what ye shall eat, or what ye shall drink; nor yet for your body, what ye shall put on. Is not the life more than meat, and the body than raiment? (Matthew 6:25).

These things I have spoken unto you, that in me ye might have peace. In the world ye shall have tribulation: but be of good cheer; I have overcome the world (John 16:33).

Casting all your care upon him; for he careth for you (1 Peter 5:7).

Worry

Lord, help me to stay calm and collected when I am faced with stressful situations. Help me to be strong and resolute in hard times. Help me to depend on You and Your strength to overcome any difficulties that come my way.

Lord Jesus, thank You for giving me Your peace, the peace that passes all understanding, peace that the world cannot comprehend. Because of that peace, I can face every situation with the confidence that You will provide a way of escape.

Lord, You told me not to let my heart be troubled. I will not give in to fear. I refuse to let myself be afraid or intimidated, because Your peace is in control of my life. I have put my confidence and trust in You, so I will not be nervous. I will not be worried or frustrated, and I will not be afraid when difficult situations come. Instead, by Your peace, Lord, I will boldly believe and say what You promised me in Your Word.

Scriptures

And the peace of God, which passeth all understanding, shall keep your hearts and minds through Christ Jesus (Philippians 4:7).

There hath no temptation taken you but such as is common to man: but God is faithful, who will not suffer you to be tempted above that ye are able; but will with the temptation also make a way to escape, that ye may be able to bear it (1 Corinthians 10:13).

Peace I leave with you, my peace I give unto you: not as the world giveth, give I unto you. Let not your heart be troubled, neither let it be afraid (John 14:27).

VI

My Relationships

Relationships

Holy Spirit, build my relationships. I ask that You would make them strong. Thanks for placing other people on the planet for me to be around. I want my relationships with people to be an offspring of my relationship with You.

Give me wisdom on the level of relationship that I should have with people. Help me to not get too close to people I am not supposed to be close to, and help me to not push away potential close friends. I need wisdom to know which people to hang out with.

Help me to point the way to You through my relationships with people. I want them to grow in their walk with You through their time with me. At the same time, I want to spend time with people who will help me to grow in my walk with You.

With my friends who are close to You, I want what You have placed inside of them to be shown to me. And in those I spend time with who do not know You well, I ask that I could influence them. I want You to be the focus.

Scriptures

A man that hath friends must shew himself friendly: and there is a friend that sticketh closer than a brother (Proverbs 18:24).

A friend loveth at all times, and a brother is born for adversity (Proverbs 17:17).

Let the word of Christ dwell in you richly in all wisdom; teaching and admonishing one another in psalms and hymns and spiritual songs, singing with grace in your hearts to the Lord (Colossians 3:16).

Creating Friendships

Jesus, let me be a light that shines You in this world. I want people to be attracted to the light inside of me. Help people to see the fruit of the Spirit that is in my life because of You.

Help them to see my love because of Your unconditional love on the cross. Help them to see my joy because knowing that You are God makes every day a celebration. Help them to see my peace because You have everything under control. Help them to see my patience because You are patient with me through my shortcomings. Help them to see my kindness because Your kindness led me to repentance. Help them to see my goodness, not because of me, but because I know a God who is extraordinarily good. Help them to see my faithfulness to You and to them because Your faithfulness to me never ends. Help them to see my gentleness, just as You so gently have bandaged my wounds. Help them to see my self-control because, through knowing You, I never have temporary feelings that get the best of me; I know that my eternal promise is much more special.

Scriptures

In the same way, let your light shine before men, that they may see your good deeds and praise your Father in heaven (Matthew 5:16).

But the fruit of the Spirit is love, joy, peace, long-suffering, gentleness, goodness, faith, meekness, temperance: against such there is no law (Galatians 5:22,23).

And this is the promise that he hath promised us, even eternal life (1 John 2:25).

Preparing for a Date

Holy Spirit, as I go out tonight, be with me. Give me peace as I go on this date. Lord, I ask that You would give me wisdom to know the right people to be around and to spend time with. Lord, as I go on dates, tell me the right places to go and the right things to do. Help me to not get caught in positions that could lead me astray. I seek to honor You through every relationship in my life. I pray that the person I'm going out with tonight would give the date to You also. Help us to have fun tonight getting to know each other. I place You at the center of my dating life. And, Lord, when You lead me to the person I will someday marry, I give that relationship to You. I know that true love is found only in You. I ask that the one I marry will reflect Your love, and that I, too, will reflect Your love. Help me to discern what is Your plan and what is not. This is the cry of my heart, Lord. I give You the date tonight.

Scriptures

If any of you lack wisdom, let him ask of God, that giveth to all men liberally, and upbraideth not; and it shall be given him (James 1:5).

A man's heart deviseth his way: but the Lord directeth his steps (Proverbs 16:9).

He that loveth not knoweth not God; for God is love (1 John 4:8).

Sexual Purity

Lord, I know that my body is Your temple. I pray for supernatural strength that can only be found in You. I know that sexual temptation is one that will be very tough to overcome. I hold on to Your promise, Jesus. I know that You have someone for me whom I will be able to share this experience with after we are married. Give me patience. Be my hope. Help me to stay away from compromising situations and to hold on to the promise of purity. Even though this is a difficult situation, Your Word says that even though I am young, I should set an example in purity. Help me to be that example for my future children and for other people in my life. I know that You told me to stay pure not just to make a rule, but because You know that my life will be better if I wait for the one You have designed for me. I cling to Your strength, Lord. Work through me. I will continue to stand as long as I hold on to You.

Scriptures

What? know ye not that your body is the temple of the Holy Ghost which is in you, which ye have of God, and ye are not your own? (1 Corinthians 6:19).

Let no man despise thy youth; but be thou an example of the believers, in word, in conversation, in charity, in spirit, in faith, in purity (1 Peter 4:12).

The Lord is my strength and my shield; my heart trusted in him, and I am helped: therefore my heart greatly rejoiceth; and with my song will I praise him (Psalm 28:7).

Breaking Up With a Boyfriend/Girlfriend

Heavenly Father, I come to You in faith asking for courage and strength to walk through this situation. I need You to comfort me and minister to me by Your Word and Your Spirit. Ending a close relationship is emotionally and physically distressing. It's difficult to address such an emotional issue in a logical or practical manner. Help me to cast the care and weight that I am feeling over on You. Help me to trust You with this transition in my life. Help me to stay focused on You and not on this problem.

My prayer is that Your will be done in my life concerning this relationship. You can see the future and You know what is best for me and for the person I was dating. If this is Your will for my life, then please make it clear to me and the person I have been dating. Confirm the decision by granting Your peace to both of us. Let our desire to fulfill Your perfect plan for our lives be greater than any emotional attachment we might have.

If breaking up was not Your will, then please guide both of us in the restoration of this relationship. If this break-up was the result of the enemy's attack, then help us recognize the source, be quick to stand against the strategies of the enemy, and quickly resolve any conflict that has resulted.

Whatever the case, I know You can and will redeem any situation in my life if I will give that situation to You. Restore to me a joyful countenance and help me to not lose my hope or joy. Help me trust You totally and completely with my life. Draw me close to You, direct my steps, and guide me as I acknowledge You in my life. Fulfill Your plan and purpose in my life.

Give me the courage and resolve to do Your will and obey Your voice in this situation.

Scriptures

Casting all your care upon him; for he careth for you (1 Peter 5:7).

I will not leave you comfortless: I will come to you (John 14:18).

If any of you lack wisdom, let him ask of God, that giveth to all men liberally, and upbraideth not; and it shall be given him. But be ye doers of the word, and not hearers only, deceiving your own selves (James 1:5,22).

Family

God, keep my relationships with my family members strong. Help us to always be there for each other, even through the tough times. Strengthen our bond as a family and help us to grow together through adversity. You have placed family in my life for a reason, even if I can't always see why. Thank You for that.

Bless my parents for raising me and training me. Keep them safe as they go through the difficult things of life. Always be with them and remind them of Your love for them. Also, remind them how much I love them, even if I may not always show it.

Bless my brothers and sisters. Thank You that they point out my mistakes and also my accomplishments. Thank You for Your purpose in each of their hearts. Keep them in Your loving arms forever, and always remind them of Your hand on their lives.

Thank You for all of the memories we've had together and for the many to come. Keep Your hand on our family. I give them to You. They're Yours.

Scriptures

Be completely humble and gentle; be patient, bearing with one another in love (Ephesians 4:2).

Honour thy father and thy mother: that thy days may be long upon the land which the Lord thy God giveth thee (Exodus 20:12).

Her children arise up, and call her blessed; her husband also, and he praiseth her (Proverbs 31:28).

Understanding My Parents

Lord, help me to understand my parents and the wisdom that they bring to my life. Help me to not reject their discipline and advice. Right now, Lord, I don't understand everything that they do. People tell me that I will appreciate them when I am older, but give me the wisdom to appreciate them now. Thanks for putting them in my life. Help us to grow closer every day. I want to be a reflection of You in my interactions with them.

At the same time, help my parents to understand me better. It's been a while since they were my age, and it is probably difficult to know everything that I am facing. Things have changed a little bit since they were my age. But help me to not write off what they do know. You have given them to me for a reason, and I do not take that for granted. I know that there is so much that I can learn from them, and there is so much that they can learn from me. Help us to communicate and spend time together so we can understand each other better. Thank You, Jesus.

Scriptures

Be completely humble and gentle; be patient, bearing with one another in love (Ephesians 4:2).

Honour thy father and thy mother: that thy days may be long upon the land which the Lord thy God giveth thee (Exodus 20:12).

Her children arise up, and call her blessed; her husband also, and he praiseth her (Proverbs 31:28).

Finding My Soul Mate

Lord, I pray for the person whom You have called to join me and walk through life with me, side by side. Be with (him/her) right now. Comfort (him/her) in (his/her) difficult times and watch over (him/her) as (he/she) sleeps. I only want the person whom You have chosen for me. Keep me away from others who are not the right one. Show me what is good for me and what is bad for me in choosing this friend for life. I want to stay on the road that *You* have for me.

I want to find someone who will love me with (his/her) whole heart and will always be there for me. I want to marry someone whose personality, vision, and purpose lines up perfectly with mine. I want someone whose relationship with You is outstanding. I want (him/her) to know You and to be extremely close to You.

Help me to be a good spouse. Help me to serve my companion always and to remain true to (him/her). Help me to not get anxious to find (him/her), but to be patient and know that You know my future spouse very well.

Scriptures

Whoso findeth a wife findeth a good thing, and obtaineth favour of the Lord (Proverbs 18:22).

Therefore shall a man leave his father and his mother, and shall cleave unto his wife: and they shall be one flesh (Genesis 2:24).

Strengthened with all might, according to his glorious power, unto all patience and longsuffering with joyfulness (Colossians 1:11).

Future Family

Lord, I give my future household to You. Help me to be a good parent and a good spouse. I see many people base their families' decisions on so many philosophies, but I make the commitment today that as for me and my house, we will serve You, Lord.

Lord, You know my children even now, before they are born. Thank You for instilling in them unique purposes. Give any sons that I might have the strength to be mighty men of valor for You. And give any daughters that I might have strength to stand against any pressures that might come their way.

Help us to be a family like none other. Help us to stand together and never forsake each other. Everything that we do, Lord, will honor and glorify Your name. Help me to know what to do and when to do it in this family. I am Your servant, Lord. No matter how big or small my family may be, I give it completely to You. You are my Savior and my King. There is no one like You.

Scriptures

And if it seem evil unto you to serve the Lord, choose you this day whom ye will serve; whether the gods which your fathers served that were on the other side of the flood, or the gods of the Amorites, in whose land ye dwell: but as for me and my house, we will serve the Lord (Joshua 24:15).

Thine eyes did see my substance, yet being unperfect; and in thy book all my members were written, which in continuance were fashioned, when as yet there was none of them (Psalm 139:16).

And there ye shall eat before the Lord your God, and ye shall rejoice in all that ye put your hand unto, ye and your households, wherein the Lord thy God hath blessed thee (Dueteronomy 12:7).

When Others Make Bad Choices

God, I don't want to get tripped up in bad choices as some of my friends do. Help me to stand strong, apart from the crowd, and follow You. I make that commitment to You today. I will not be swayed by the opinions of others, but will stand with You.

I will stand alone, but thank You that I'm not alone. You are always with me. I don't need to listen to the voices of other people, because I hear Your voice. Lord, give me strength to overcome the temptations of having sex before I'm married, doing drugs, drinking, and smoking. I know that the reason You don't want me to do these things is that You know they are bad for me. It hurts You when I hurt myself.

Thank You that I am in the world, but not of the world. I will not conform to the world's patterns, but to a relationship with You. A relationship with You is so much better than anything the world could offer. Help me to not be like the others who reject You, but give me strength and a constant reminder of Your love.

Scriptures

And be not conformed to this world: but be ye transformed by the renewing of your mind, that ye may prove what is that good, and acceptable, and perfect, will of God (Romans 12:2).

For all that is in the world, the lust of the flesh, and the lust of the eyes, and the pride of life, is not of the Father, but is of the world (1 John 2:16).

But I will sing of thy power; yea, I will sing aloud of thy mercy in the morning: for thou hast been my defence and refuge in the day of my trouble (Psalm 59:16).

Sharing God's Love

Lord, thank You for Your love that You poured out on the cross. Help me to pour out that love every day. When people do things to hurt me, help me to not react out of my emotions, but to make the decision to show Your love to them.

When I come across people who have no friends, help me to reach out to them and be a friend to them, pointing them to You. Thank You, Lord, that You were a friend to the friendless. When someone talks bad about me, help me to have the strength to respond completely in love, without bitterness or anger.

At the same time, help me to not talk behind people's backs, to not gossip about others. Always remind me of Your love. Remind me of the responsibility that You have given me to show that love to others. I make the commitment to You that I will share Your love. I offer myself and my life to You as a living sacrifice. Help me to love my neighbor as myself.

Scriptures

Let no man despise thy youth; but be thou an example of the believers, in word, in conversation, in charity, in spirit, in faith, in purity (1 Timothy 4:12).

I beseech you therefore, brethren, by the mercies of God, that ye present your bodies a living sacrifice, holy, acceptable unto God, which is your reasonable service (Romans 12:1).

Thou shalt love the Lord thy God with all thy heart, and with all thy soul, and with all thy strength, and with all thy mind; and thy neighbour as thyself (Luke 10:27).

For Leaders in My Life

Lord, I pray for the leaders You have placed over me. Give them wisdom, and order their steps in Your ways.

I pray for my bosses at work. Let them make the right decisions and always treat their employees with respect.

I pray for the leaders in my school. As my principal oversees all the decisions that are made in my school, help him to honor You and do what is best for the students. I pray that all of the administrators would make caring for the students their primary goal. Lord, I pray for my teachers. Give them wisdom to teach the material well and with understanding. Help them to realize the importance of their jobs: that they are not only teaching us but making a lasting impact on our lives.

I pray for the ministers at my church. I know that it must be difficult to shepherd Your people. Give them peace and strength to stand. Help them to know that they are making a difference. I pray for my youth ministers. Help them to know what each of the kids need and how to meet each need through Your love.

Scriptures

I exhort therefore, that, first of all, supplications, prayers, intercessions, and giving of thanks, be made for all men; for kings, and for all that are in authority; that we may lead a quiet and peaceable life in all godliness and honesty (1 Timothy 2:1,2).

Put them in mind to be subject to principalities and powers, to obey magistrates, to be ready to every good work (Titus 3:1).

Let every soul be subject unto the higher powers. For there is no power but of God: the powers that be are ordained of God (Romans 13:1).

VII

My Every Day

Living on My Own

Lord, it is very difficult to be away from the things and the people that mean the most to me and are the most familiar to me. Please give me strength to make it on my own. I need Your peace and Your guidance.

Help me to realize that my home is found in You. You are my shelter, the place where I can find rest. When I am scared and alone, You are there to comfort me. Even when I've had a bad day and I feel that the world is against me, help me to know that You are there for me.

Help my family, as I know that this is a difficult time for them as well as for me. Give them peace and everlasting joy. Give me wisdom in knowing how to survive without the familiar things. Show me the best way to organize my time, do the laundry, and make my meals. Thank You that we are in this together. I don't have to do it on my own. You are the best friend that I could ever have, and my awesome Father.

Scriptures

God is our refuge and strength, a very present help in trouble (Psalm 46:1).

And my people shall dwell in a peaceable habitation, and in sure dwellings, and in quiet resting places (Isaiah 32:18).

A man that hath friends must shew himself friendly: and there is a friend that sticketh closer than a brother (Proverbs 18:24).

To Find a Job

God, I don't know what to do. I need Your direction to find a job. Lord, I just ask that You would find the job that is right for me and bring it to me. You know my needs, and You know the right way to meet them. Make it obvious, in my time with You, what I am supposed to do. Lord, I need You.

Lord, please send me to an employer who is going to see the special things that You have placed inside of me and use them to the highest potential. Help me to be a light where I work. Lord, I don't just want a job—I want to be exactly where You want me to be.

Help me to show You to any customers or clients I encounter. I want others to ask me what is so special about me. I want them to ask why I am so joyful. Then I will tell them that it is because of You. Lord, I commit my entire job situation to You and Your kingdom.

Scriptures

As every man hath received the gift, even so minister the same one to another, as good stewards of the manifold grace of God (1 Peter 4:10).

...your Father knoweth what things ye have need of, before ye ask him (Matthew 6:8).

Trust in the Lord with all thine heart; and lean not unto thine own understanding. In all thy ways acknowledge him, and he shall direct thy paths (Proverbs 3:5,6).

Finding the Right Church

Lord, help me to find a church that fits who You have made me to be. I want to find a church where I am fed with Your Word every week. Help me to find a church with a pastor who cares for me and wants to see me grow in You. I ask that this church would have activities appropriate for my age and people whom I can connect with. Thank You for fellowship with other believers, and the power of coming together.

Help me to find a church that teaches Your Word as its only source of absolute truth. I ask that You keep me away from false doctrine and people who do not place You as Creator and King. Lord, help me to enjoy going to church and to be excited about what I experience there.

When I do find the right church, give me opportunities to serve You in a greater way. I desire to find a church where I don't just sit to be entertained, but where I can participate in the church body. I know that You will show me where I am supposed to be in Your time.

Scriptures

Not forsaking the assembling of ourselves together, as the manner of some is; but exhorting one another: and so much the more, as ye see the day approaching (Hebrews 10:25).

Each one should use whatever gift he has received to serve others, faithfully administering God's grace in its various forms (1 Peter 4:10).

A man's heart deviseth his way: but the Lord directeth his steps (Proverbs 16:9).

Now What?

You have been such a good God. Thank You for Your blessings and for just keeping me going. Lord, now I face what is ahead. But I'm scared because I don't even know what is ahead. My mind, at times, tries to figure everything out about my future rather than trusting You. Help me to trust You, Lord. Even when things are uncertain, I want to trust You. You can see everything that has happened and everything that will happen. And You will tell me in Your perfect timing. I am not worried because You are in control.

Help me to not make decisions based on stress or concern, but on the wisdom that You have given me. In the Bible, Solomon asked for wisdom before anything else. That is my prayer, Lord. Give me wisdom for whatever my future holds.

Every day I see something new about who You are, God. I don't want to focus each day on the concerns of life. Instead, I want to focus on what new thing I am going to learn about Jesus today. Your mercies are new every morning, Jesus. Thanks for looking out for me.

Scriptures

The Lord will fulfill his purpose for me; your love, O Lord, endures forever... (Psalm 138:8).

And God said to Solomon, Because this was in thine heart, and thou hast not asked riches, wealth, or honour, nor the life of thine enemies, neither yet hast asked long life; but hast asked wisdom and knowledge for thyself, that thou mayest judge my people, over whom I have made thee king (2 Chronicles 1:11).

It is of the Lord's mercies that we are not consumed, because his compassions fail not. They are new every morning: great is thy faithfulness (Lamentations 3:22,23).

Moving to a New Area

Lord, I need a friend in my life. I feel like I am leaving all of my security at home. But I know that You are the best security that I could ask for. Stay with me, Lord Jesus. At times I might get lonely. Please be my comfort.

And, Lord, I ask that You would bring new, close friends into my life who love and honor You. I don't want to be closed off to new opportunities and experiences that You have for me. I get a little concerned that the people in the new place won't like me. But, Lord, my focus is not that they would like me. I just want to show You to them through my life.

Thanks for Your confidence because I know who I am in You. You call me Your child and Your friend. Keep me safe from harm, and watch over my friends at home. Thank You for the relationships that I have with them, and thank You for the new opportunities ahead.

Scriptures

But let all who take refuge in you be glad; let them ever sing for joy. Spread your protection over them, that those who love your name may rejoice in you (Psalm 5:11).

God is our refuge and strength, a very present help in trouble (Psalm 46:1).

For a great door and effectual is opened unto me (1 Corinthians 16:9).

Transition

Holy Spirit, walk me through the transitions that I am about to go through. I know that it may be tough, but with You nothing is too difficult. I know that You are my counselor, and You have been called along my side to see me through the tough times. I know that this change is good for me, and no matter how many times that I am shaken, I will not break because You are my God. Mold me into Your image, Father. Make me strong in You. Who I am in You is not based on my surroundings, but on what You say about me. And You think that I am awesome.

Help me with the changes.

Things may seem new to me, but I know that You are always the same. People may treat me differently, but I know that You will always love me and see me as valuable. My activities may change, but let's always keep our time together. My personality, dress, and speech may even change, but Your purpose inside of me will never change.

Scriptures

For with God nothing shall be impossible (Luke 1:37).

And I will pray the Father, and he shall give you another Comforter, that he may abide with you for ever (John 14:16).

Jesus Christ is the same yesterday and today and forever (Hebrews 13:8).

Travel

Lord, keep me safe as I travel. Give me Your traveling mercies on the trip that I am about to take. Thank You for Your peace so that I am not worried about what could happen but am secure in Your arms of protection surrounding my vehicle.

I ask that You would keep me way from turbulent weather and from any accident that the enemy would try to throw in my direction. I know that everything in heaven and on earth is Yours, so You have control over everything. I have peace in the fact that You are God. There is no limit to Your control: no matter where I am in the world.

Where could I go from Your presence? Everywhere I go, You are there. Even when I am far away, You are there. Your eye is even on the smallest sparrow. How much more is it on me? I let go of all of the potential stress of traveling. It's not worth worrying about. Help me to enjoy my trip, and help me to know You more through my journey.

Scriptures

Whither shall I go from thy spirit? or whither shall I flee from thy presence? .... Even there shall thy hand lead me, and thy right hand shall hold me (Psalm 139:7,10).

Are not five sparrows sold for two farthings, and not one of them is forgotten before God?
But even the very hairs of your head are all numbered. Fear not therefore: ye are of more value than many sparrows (Luke 12:6,7).

Have not I commanded thee? Be strong and of a good courage; be not afraid, neither be thou dismayed: for the Lord thy God is with thee whithersoever thou goest (Joshua 1:9).

Money

Dear Father, I know that it is Your will to bless me. I know that as I am faithful to pay my tithes and give to Your work, You will bless me. You said that as I give it shall be given back to me, good measure, pressed down, and shaken together.

Your Word says that You love a cheerful giver. Help me to be sensitive to Your Spirit, and help me to be obedient to give as You instruct me. Give me wisdom and understanding, that I might be a good steward over all that You have given me. Help me to use discretion in my spending habits. Let me be practical, sensible, and intelligent in all my buying decisions.

Give me creative ideas and new insight to create income for my family. Help me to be productive and diligent in my job. Give me favor with my employer.

I thank You, Lord, that increase and promotion come from You. I thank You that I and my family are blessed. Let us be financially successful so that we can be abundant givers to Your work and a blessing to others.

Scriptures

Bring ye all the tithes into the storehouse, that there may be meat in mine house, and prove me now herewith, saith the Lord of hosts, if I will not open you the windows of heaven, and pour you out a blessing, that there shall not be room enough to receive it (Malachi 3:10).

Every man according as he purposeth in his heart, so let him give; not grudgingly, or of necessity: for God loveth a cheerful giver (2 Corinthians 9:7).

He that diligently seeketh good procureth favour: but he that seeketh mischief, it shall come unto him (Proverbs 11:27).

For promotion cometh neither from the east, nor from the west, nor from the south. But God is the judge: he putteth down one, and setteth up another (Proverbs 75:6,7).

Giving

Lord, thanks for blessing me with the joyful opportunity to give to Your kingdom. Everything I have comes from You. It is a privilege to give money and resources to Your work so that others might hear the good news of the Gospel.

Lord, I don't give to get; I give to honor You and to be a blessing to others. Your Word says that if I am faithful to give of my substance, then You will bless me and my family. Thank You for providing for my every need. I thank You that as I tithe, You open the windows of heaven and pour out abundant and overwhelming blessings on me.

You promised to rebuke the devourer for my sake. You promised that whatever I do for others You would make happen for me. You said that the righteous would never have to beg for what we need. You promised that with whatever measure I give You would cause others to give to me.

I thank You that as I am faithful to pay my tithes and give offering to Your work, You bless me with abundant financial provision.

Scriptures

Honour the Lord with thy substance, and with the firstfruits of all thine increase (Proverbs 3:9).

Bring ye all the tithes into the storehouse, that there may be meat in mine house, and prove me now herewith, saith the Lord of hosts, if I will not open you the windows of heaven, and pour you out a blessing, that there shall not be room enough to receive it. And I will rebuke the devourer for your sakes, and he shall not destroy the fruits of your ground; neither shall your vine cast her fruit before the time in the field, saith the Lord of hosts (Malachi 3:10,11).

Give, and it shall be given unto you; good measure, pressed down, and shaken together, and running over, shall men give into your bosom. For with the same measure that ye mete withal it shall be measured to you again (Luke 6:38).

VIII

My Nation

The Nation

Lord, thank You for freedom. Thank You for the opportunity to live in a nation like ours. Thank You for founding fathers who loved You and followed Your ways. Help us to return to our Christian ways. We know that when we seek You first, everything else will follow.

I pray for our leaders. Give them wisdom to see Your ways. Give our president and vice president the ability to discern the right and wrong decisions and the strength to stand for values and morals that line up with Your Word. I pray for Congress. Thank You for the power of diversity and the power of teamwork. Help them to make decisions that are inspired only by You. I pray for all the cabinet members and other leaders in the country. I pray for a further realization of who You are and what Your unfailing love can do for this nation.

Help us to return to You, Jesus. That is the cry of our hearts. Help my generation to rise up seeing You as the only way. Give us the strength to fight for true freedom, Your freedom, because where Your Spirit is there is true liberty.

Scriptures

But seek ye first the kingdom of God, and his righteousness; and all these things shall be added unto you (Matthew 6:33).

Now the Lord is that Spirit: and where the Spirit of the Lord is, there is liberty (2 Corinthians 3:17).

And it shall come to pass in the last days, saith God, I will pour out of my Spirit upon all flesh: and your sons and your daughters shall prophesy, and your young men shall see visions, and your old men shall dream dreams (Acts 2:17).

The President

Dear Father, in Jesus' name, I lift up our nation's president to You. I know that our leader's heart is in Your hand, so I ask You to guide him in the way You want him to go.

Give our president spiritual, physical, and mental strength to fulfill his responsibilities with excellence. Give him the courage to stand up for his convictions. Give him patience and peace to endure the pressures of his office.

Help him to be determined to do the right thing no matter how much pressure he feels from those who oppose him. Give our president wisdom and insight concerning every decision that he must make. Make him bold to lead our nation with integrity and honor.

I pray that You would give our president discernment, understanding, and knowledge so that our nation may know stability, both internally and abroad.

I pray that You would surround our president with wise counsel, godly men and women of integrity who place Your agenda and the good of this nation above their own, people whose motives are pure, honest, and trustworthy.

I pray for our president's family. Encourage and strengthen their spirits, souls, and bodies. Protect them from evil and harm. Help them to be supportive of the president, and give them strength to deal with the pressures and demands of being the First Family.

Thanks for our president and thanks for working through his leadership so that we can live peacefully in godliness and honesty.

Scriptures

The king's heart is in the hand of the Lord, as the rivers of water: he turneth it whithersoever he will (Proverbs 21:1).

Praying always with all prayer and supplication in the Spirit, and watching thereunto with all perseverance and supplication for all saints; and for me, that utterance may be given unto me, that I may open my mouth boldly, to make known the mystery of the gospel, for which I am an ambassador in bonds: that therein I may speak boldly, as I ought to speak (Ephesians 6:18-20).

I exhort therefore, that, first of all, supplications, prayers, intercessions, and giving of thanks, be made for all men; for kings, and for all that are in authority; that we may lead a quiet and peaceable life in all godliness and honesty (1 Timothy 2:1,2).

Congress

Dear Father, in Jesus' name, thank You for our great nation. Thank You for the plan You gave to our forefathers to govern our nation and to divide the powers so that our destiny would not rest in the hands of one person.

Your Word tells me to pray for those in authority, so I lift up our Congress—both the House of Representatives and the Senate. I pray that by Your power, our federal legislative body will make laws that are just.

Father, I ask You to give them wisdom to make decisions that would strengthen and prosper our nation. Enlighten them with Your truth so that they make right decisions concerning the politics, the social welfare, and the economics of our nation.

Help the members of Congress to put aside personal and party-line agendas and to work together with others for the good of our nation. Help them to work with the president so together they can introduce and pass legislation that strengthens our nation and supports the godly values of our society.

I pray for revival in Congress. Draw the representatives of our United States close to You, Lord. Give those who know You the courage to vote their convictions and to be bold witnesses for You. For those who don't have a personal relationship with You, I pray that the eyes of their understanding will be opened and their hearts turned toward You.

Scriptures

I exhort therefore, that, first of all, supplications, prayers, intercessions, and giving of thanks, be made for all men; for kings, and for all that are in authority; that we may lead a quiet and peaceable life in all godliness and honesty (1 Timothy 2:1,2).

Therefore he said unto Judah, Let us build these cities, and make about them walls, and towers, gates, and bars, while the land is yet before us; because we have sought the Lord our God, we have sought him, and he hath given us rest on every side. So they built and prospered (2 Chronicles 14:7).

The eyes of your understanding being enlightened; that ye may know what is the hope of his calling, and what the riches of the glory of his inheritance in the saints (Ephesians 1:18).

The Military

Thank You, Lord, for the men and women of our armed forces. Protect them as they protect us. Defend them as they defend us. Encourage and strengthen their spirits, souls, and bodies as they perform their duties. Make them mentally and physically strong when they have to face the challenges of combat. Reveal to them the truth and knowledge of Your will for their lives. Help them to be successful in their endeavors, spare their lives from destruction, and deliver them from harm's way.

May our response to any aggression by enemies of this nation be swift, accurate, and effective. Reveal the plans, plots, and strategies of our enemies to our military intelligence personnel. Confuse our enemies, and let them become disorganized and disoriented regarding their battle plans.

Father, give our military favor with the government. Thank You for providing America with the best-trained and best-equipped military force in the world today. I pray that our Congress would appropriate sufficient funds to keep our nation's military preeminent in the world.

Scriptures

The king's heart is in the hand of the Lord, as the rivers of water: he turneth it whithersoever he will (Proverbs 21:1).

Confuse the wicked, O Lord, confound their speech, for I see violence and strife in the city (Psalm 55:9).

He keepeth the paths of judgment, and preserveth the way of his saints (Proverbs 2:8).

National Patriotism

Lord, thank You for the United States of America. Thank You for the dedication, faith, and courage of our founding fathers. Thank You for the patriotism of the generations that have gone before us. Thank You for those brave patriots who have shed their blood for my freedom. Lord, thank You for all the families who have sacrificed so much so that we can enjoy the liberty we now have.

I pray for the people of this generation. Help us to regain the spirit of patriotism that once was so much a part of every American. May our hearts be full of compassion and thankfulness every time we see our flag or hear our national anthem.

I pray that Christians would vote for and elect godly officials. Help us to prayerfully support those who are in authority.

Restore to our nation godly character. Promote to positions of authority leaders who will honor You. Let revival and spiritual restoration sweep our country.

Scriptures

I exhort therefore, that, first of all, supplications, prayers, intercessions, and giving of thanks, be made for all men; for kings, and for all that are in authority; that we may lead a quiet and peaceable life in all godliness and honesty (1 Timothy 2:1,2).

When the righteous are in authority, the people rejoice: but when the wicked beareth rule, the people mourn (Proverbs 29:2).

But it is God who judges: He brings one down, he exalts another (Psalm 75:7).

And it shall come to pass in the last days, saith God, I will pour out of my Spirit upon all flesh: and your sons and your daughters shall prophesy, and your young men shall see visions, and your old men shall dream dreams (Acts 2:17).

National Protection

God, I ask You for divine protection for the people of this nation. I pray for the safety of every person here. Keep us from harm's way, and protect us from the plans of destruction that our enemies have plotted. Stop our enemies' strategies of destruction.

Give wisdom, understanding, and discernment to the people who provide protection. Help us as citizens to be watchful and alert to signs of wrongdoing.

Give insight and ideas to inventors and scientists to create better ways to protect our country from financial, political, and mental espionage and terrorism.

Provide insight to national and local authorities to guard, defend, and ensure the safety of all American citizens, both at home and abroad. Help us to unite with government leaders and law enforcement personnel to make this country a safe place to live, work, and play.

Scriptures

If my people, which are called by my name, shall humble themselves, and pray, and seek my face, and turn from their wicked ways; then will I hear from heaven, and will forgive their sin, and will heal their land (2 Chronicles 7:14).

I exhort therefore, that, first of all, supplications, prayers, intercessions, and giving of thanks, be made for all men; for kings, and for all that are in authority; that we may lead a quiet and peaceable life in all godliness and honesty (1 Timothy 2:1,2).

Watch and pray, that ye enter not into temptation: the spirit indeed is willing, but the flesh is weak (Matthew 26:41).

In Time of War

Father, I come to You in Jesus' name concerning the war effort that our nation is currently undertaking. Give wisdom, insight, and direction to our president and military leaders who are making decisions pertaining to the war.

Reveal the plans, strategies, and inside information about our enemies to our military intelligence personnel. Confuse our enemies. Let them become disorganized and disoriented regarding their battle plans.

I pray that You protect each one of our military personnel involved in the war. Send Your angels to protect them, and go with them to keep them from harm and injury. Encourage and strengthen our armed forces in their spirits, souls, and bodies. Lead them into the truth and knowledge of Your will for their lives. Help them to be successful in their endeavors, spare their lives from destruction, and deliver them from harm's way.

Scriptures

I exhort therefore, that, first of all, supplications, prayers, intercessions, and giving of thanks, be made for all men; for kings, and for all that are in authority; that we may lead a quiet and peaceable life in all godliness and honesty (1 Timothy 2:1,2).

Confuse the wicked, O Lord, confound their speech, for I see violence and strife in the city (Psalm 55:9).

For he shall give his angels charge over thee, to keep thee in all thy ways (Psalm 91:11).

But let all who take refuge in you be glad; let them ever sing for joy. Spread your protection over them, that those who love your name may rejoice in you (Psalm 5:11).

God is our refuge and strength, a very present help in trouble (Psalm 46:1).

Prayer of Salvation

God loves you—no matter who you are, no matter what your past. God loves you so much that He gave His one and only begotten Son for you. The Bible tells us that "...whoever believes in him shall not perish but have eternal life" (John 3:16 NIV). Jesus laid down His life and rose again so that we could spend eternity with Him in heaven and experience His absolute best on earth. If you would like to receive Jesus into your life, say the following prayer out loud and mean it from your heart.

Heavenly Father, I come to You admitting that I am a sinner. Right now, I choose to turn away from sin, and I ask You to cleanse me of all unrighteousness. I believe that Your Son, Jesus, died on the cross to take away my sins. I also believe that He rose again from the dead so that I might be forgiven of my sins and made righteous through faith in Him. I call upon the name of Jesus Christ to be the Savior and Lord of my life. Jesus, I choose to follow You and ask that You fill me with the power of the Holy Spirit. I declare that right now I am a child of God. I am free from sin and full of the right-eousness of God. I am saved in Jesus' name. Amen.

If you prayed this prayer to receive Jesus Christ as your Savior for the first time, please contact us on the web at www.whitestonebooks.com to receive a free book.

Or you may write to us at
White Stone Books
P.O. Box 35035
Tulsa, Oklahoma 74153

Other Books by White Stone

Scriptural Prayers for the Praying Woman

Scriptural Prayers for the Praying Man

Scriptural Prayers for the Praying Mother

Additional copies of this book
are available from your local bookstore.

WHITE STONE BOOKS
TULSA, OKLAHOMA

The White Stone Vision

To publish inspirational books

Which contain the eternal principles of God's Word

And encourage readers to draw near to God,

To experience His love and grace,

And to glorify the Lord Jesus Christ.

"He who has an ear, let him hear what the Spirit says
to the churches. To him who overcomes I will give some
of the hidden manna to eat. And I will give him a
white stone, and on the stone a new name written
which no one knows except him who receives it"'
(Revelation 2:17)